Best wish...

The Brontës by

Including Walks

Rhonda Petersen

An account of Charlotte and Anne Brontë's
visits to the East and North Yorkshire Coast

Line drawings by David Winter

Rhonda Peter...

Bridlington Quay

Published by Bretlington Publishing (Bridlington) 1997

Charlotte Brontë painted in 1855 by J H Thompson

Reproduction courtesy of the Brontë Society

Acknowledgements:
The Brontë Society Library for advice and help
Bridlington Library for help
Mike Wilson - grateful thanks for help and encouragement
Hilda Slater for help
Michael Thornton for help

Illustrations:
David Winter for line drawings
Peter Hornby for photograph of Easton Farmhouse

Photographs:
Rhonda Peterson

Principal Sources:
The Life of Charlotte Brontë - Mrs E Gaskell 1857
Bridlington-Quay - Thomas Cape 1877
The Three Brontës - May Sinclair 1930
The Clue to the Brontës - G. Elsie Harrison 1948
The Four Brontës - Lawrence and E.M.Hanson 1949
The Brontë Sisters - Phyllis Bentley 1950
Charlotte Brontë on the E .Yorkshire Coast - F.R. Pearson 1952
Charlotte Brontë - Kevin Berry 1990
The Brontës - Juliet Barker 1994
Amazing Race - Maureen Robinson 1997

ISBN   0 9530841 0 8

Published by **Bretlington Publishing** (Bridlington)
40 Wellington Road
Bridlington   YO15 2BG
Telephone: (01262) 603054

Cover & Title pages printed by
Bridlington Printing & Office Supplies
55 Wellington Road
Bridlington YO15 2AX
Telephone: 01262 400576

Cover Picture: Sea-wall Parade Bridlington 1872

Bridlington C.1848

FARM HOUSE AT EASTON

(From a Water-colour Drawing by Charlotte Brontë

Anne Brontë from a miniature painted by Charlotte Brontë

Index of Walks

Ordnance Survey Landranger Map 101 covers all walks, except Hornsea - 107

Index of Chapters   Page

Introduction

The famous Brontë sisters, all remarkable novelists, are invariably associated with West Yorkshire and the hilly town of Haworth with its parsonage and nearby wild, rolling moors. But the North and East Yorkshire coastline, with its sandy shores and impressive cliffs overlooking the North Sea, also played an important part in the lives of two of the sisters. While Emily was something of a stay at home, Charlotte and Anne developed a deep and lasting affection for the sea. It's not hard to imagine how these feelings arose when you journey to this lovely coast. Here you will find not only scenic beauty, but also clusters of grand terraced houses in Bridlington, Filey and Scarborough, reminding us of how these spa towns in their heyday drew the gentry from inland during the summer. Settings in two of the novels, *'Agnes Grey'* and *'Villette'*, also drew their inspiration from the seaside towns.

The diminutive Charlotte - she was 4'9", explored the area most thoroughly, returning four times in all. She visited Bridlington, Scarborough, Hornsea, Filey and many of the smaller villages. Anne was so passionate about the coast that she begged to be taken to her beloved Scarborough in 1849, when she almost certainly knew she was dying, to make her last bonding with the sea. She lies in the graveyard of St Mary's Church in Scarborough. Branwell, the brother remembered more for his artistic ability and his feckless lifestyle than his written work, also spent at least one summer 'season' in Scarborough. It is without doubt that the Brontës' memories of staying at the seaside reflected some of the happiest periods of their lives.

The sea was also to serve as a salve for Charlotte's heartbreak and health in later years, when, steeped in the deep sadness she endured at losing all her family save her father by the age of thirty- six, she strolled alone in the coastal towns. These escapes to the coast also helped her to get down to completing her last novels *'Shirley'* and *'Villette'*.

The tragic lives of the Brontës were as harrowing as any novel they themselves might have written. In *'The Brontës by the Sea'* I have set out to explore an important part of these lives. As a resident of East Yorkshire, I share with them a deep love of one of the most beautiful areas of England. I hope you enjoy both the book and the walks.

Rhonda Petersen

Chronology

1816 -   Charlotte born 21st April at Thornton.

1817 -   Patrick Branwell born 26th June at Thornton.

1818 -   Emily Jane born 30th July at Thornton.

1820 -   Anne born 17th January at Thornton.

1820 -   Rev. Patrick Brontë appointed to Haworth Church.

1821 -   Maria (mother) Brontë dies aged 38 at Haworth Parsonage.

1822 -   Aunt Elizabeth Branwell joins the family to help.

1825 -   Maria (junior) and Elizabeth Brontë die aged 11 & 10.

1826 -   Four remaining children schooled at home.

1831 -   Charlotte goes to Miss Wooler's school at Roe Head.
         She befriends Ellen Nussey and Mary Taylor.

1835 -   Emily a pupil at Roe Head school.

1836 -   Anne a pupil at Roe Head school.

1839 -   Anne becomes a governess at Mirfield, Charlotte at Stonegappe.
   -   September, Charlotte and Ellen Nussey holiday in Bridlington.

1840 -   Anne becomes a governess at Thorp Green.

1841 - 1845 Anne spends the summers in Scarborough.

1842 -   February. Charlotte and Emily go to Pensionnat Heger, Brussels.
   -   Aunt Branwell dies and they return to Haworth in November.

1843 -   January. Charlotte returns to Brussels, but leaves in December.
   -   Branwell becomes tutor to Robinsons' son at Thorp Green.

1845 -   Arthur Bell Nicholls appointed curate at Haworth.
   -   Anne leaves her governess post, Branwell dismissed.

1847 -   *Jane Eyre, Wuthering Heights* and *Agnes Grey* published.

1848 -   *Tenant of Wildfell Hall* by Anne published.
   -   Branwell dies aged 31 and Emily dies aged 30.

1849 -   May, Scarborough. Anne dies aged 29 on 28th May with Charlotte
         and Ellen present. Charlotte and Ellen stay in Filey and
         Bridlington. *Shirley* by Charlotte published.

1852 -   May/June. Charlotte visits Scarborough and Filey alone.

1853 -   *Villette* published. Hornsea.Charlotte visits Miss Wooler, Sept.

1854 -   Charlotte marries Rev. Arthur Bell Nicholls.

1855 -   Charlotte dies on 31st March aged 38.

1857 -   Mrs Gaskell's *Life of Charlotte Brontë* and *The Professor* by
         Charlotte published.

1861 -   Patrick Brontë, cared for by Arthur Nicholls, dies aged 84.

1897 -   Ellen Nussey dies aged 80.

Chapter 1
Bridlington, 1839

Charlotte was the first of the Brontë sisters to venture to the coast. To place the period in context, this was the time when the British Empire was at its peak. It was barely two years since the young Queen Victoria had come to the throne, New Zealand was about to be annexed, and the Opium Wars in China had just begun. The industrial revolution was in full gear and Britain's cities were centres of sordid squalor. Haworth was a town of woollen mills and grinding poverty and the Brontë sisters were amongst those few residents who were educated to a high level. Their father Patrick had procured a lifetime curacy at the church in Haworth and this small hilltop town is where the three sisters were to spend most of their short lives.

Charlotte, Emily and Jane were all employed as governesses at various points in their lives. Strong-willed Emily loathed the job, Charlotte endured it and it was only the gentler Anne who seemed to have derived some enjoyment from teaching young children. It should be remembered that in the middle of last century there were few other occupations open to educated young women of their class who needed to earn a living. It was after one such brief attachment to a family during May, June and July in 1839 that Charlotte took a holiday in Bridlington. During her three months as a nursery governess to the Sidgwick children of Stonegappe near Skipton in North Yorkshire she complained in letters that she found life there 'tedious' and 'restraining' and that she longed to escape. In a letter to Ellen Nussey, her close friend from schooldays at Roe Head school, she declared she would rather 'work in a mill' and called the Sidgwick children 'pampered' and 'turbulent'. Her extreme shyness meant she found it difficult to mix with house guests and she admitted to at times 'feeling depressed'. And she especially hated the piles of sewing, a task which alerted her to the drudgery which the role of a wife entailed. It was with great relief, then, that Charlotte returned to the Haworth parsonage and the moors she loved so much. Anxious about what her next direction in life might be, she felt very much in need of a holiday. Writing to Ellen on 26th July, she declared she 'never was so glad to get out of a house in my life'. At this time Ellen, who lived some twenty five miles from Haworth at Brookroyd House near Birstall, was planning a trip to the coast for her health. With her usual kindness, Ellen decided to invite Charlotte along, to raise her spirits. Charlotte, now twenty three years old, felt a failure; she had ambition and really wanted to suceed in something but felt that life as a private governess was 'no existence' and that a governess was 'not considered as a living and rational being, except as connected with the wearisome duties she has to fulfill.' She jumped at the chance to go away, writing to Ellen in response - 'Your proposal has driven me "clean daft" .....The fact is, an excursion with you anywhere, whether to Cleathorpe (now Cleethorpes) or Canada, just by ourselves, would be most delightful.' Later in the same letter, however, her hopes seemed to have been dashed when she added a p.s. that, 'aunt and papa have determined to go to Liverpool for a fortnight, and take us all with them.'

The young Queen Victoria around 1840.

The Liverpool trip turned out to be little more than a red herring which had been hastily thought up by Patrick Brontë and his sister, Aunt Branwell, to steer Charlotte's thoughts from her 'giddy plans' to go away with Ellen. They believed the young women would need a chaperone for such a long journey, far from the two hour dash it is today. They did their best to dissuade Charlotte but she was adamant and, when she wrote to Ellen again on 6th August, she was wildly excited by the prospect of the trip. She said that she knew that the Liverpool journey had never been more than 'a mere castle in the air' and that she had gained permission to accompany Ellen 'for a week - at the utmost, a fortnight - but no more.' She continued, - ' Where do you wish to go? Burlington (Bridlington), I should think, from what Mary (Mary Taylor, a schoolfriend) says, would be as eligible a place as any....When do you set off?' Later in the letter she eagerly imagines what the sea, which she had never seen, might be like.

'The idea of seeing the sea - of being near it - watching its changes by sunrise, sunset, moonlight, and noonday - in calm, perhaps in storm - fills and satisfies my mind. I shall be discontented at nothing.'

The pair finally settled on Bridlington as their destination, partly on their friend Mary Taylor's recommendation and partly because, in 1838, Henry (Ellen's brother) had been a curate in Burton Agnes, six miles from Bridlington, under the vicar Charles Lutwidge (the uncle of Charles Lutwidge Dodgson/Lewis Carroll, author of *Alice Through the Looking Glass'*). Henry had many friends in the area and, unbeknown to them, had arranged for the young women to stay with his friends Mr and Mrs Hudson who lived in a farmhouse at Easton, a small hamlet a couple of miles inland from Bridlington 'Quay'. Henry was a good friend of Charlotte's, and he bore no hard feelings after her firm dismissal of his lighthearted proposal of marriage in February or March of the same year. She had taken his offer seriously, and written quite frankly to him, explaining how she believed them to be unsuited. She said this was due to her strong character and that she didn't feel she could make him happy, adding that she would rather 'become an old maid' than make the wrong choice of a husband. She also suspected, quite rightly, that Henry wanted someone to look after him, and this was a role, she had learnt during her bad experiences of being a governess, she felt she was not yet prepared to take on. Henry was a humourless and solemn young curate and he was hoping to take on pupils in his house, so he was looking for a housekeeper.Only briefly when Charlotte was miserable at Stonegappe had she regretted turning him down. Now she remembered his offer with laughter. And she was right in suspecting his motives. He very quickly proposed to two others within the next year. Imagine the loss to literature had she accepted!

The steep hill in Haworth which leads up to the Parsonage.

And so the palaver of planning the journey had begun, a full two months before the young women set out for the East Riding. With no telephones, the possibility of meeting Ellen in Leeds where they would catch the train to Selby was discussed at length in letters. Charlotte worried over how to travel by coach from Keighley to Bradford in time for the Leeds train. Pigot's Directory of the time states, 'Coaches leave the Fleece Inn (Keighley) every morning at 7, then go through Bradford to Leeds every morning except Sunday at 9.' She also suggested an alternative plan whereby she might link up with Ellen at her home in Birstall and set out from there. And, just like young women of today, she agonised - 'What luggage will you take? much or little?'

Their plans were thwarted in early August when Charlotte hastily wrote to Ellen begging for more time to prepare. She was unable to get to Leeds by 10 in the morning. 'Haworth... is such an out-of-the-way place,' she complained, 'one should have a month's warning before they stir from it.' She decided to implement the Birstall plan in mid-August but again things went wrong. With her box packed and ready, she discovered that the one and only gig out of Haworth to Bradford wasn't operating. Her father and aunt wouldn't hear of her walking from Harrogate, which was the nearest coach stage to Birstall. At this point Charlotte very nearly gave up completely on the holiday, writing to Ellen on 14th August to say, 'I have in vain packed my box ...impediments seem to throw up at every step....leave me out of your calculations'. But at last, at the beginning of September, Ellen made a decision to take the bull by the horns and, borrowing her brother Henry's coach, travelled to Haworth to arrive on the parsonage doorstep with no warning. Patrick Brontë and Aunt Branwell were so surprised that they had no time to object and Charlotte hastily threw a few more things into a box and was quickly borne off in the direction of Leeds, no doubt with a good deal of giggling. And so began the great adventure. The train journey must have been terribly exciting for Charlotte - this was her first journey on the railways. 1836 - 44 was the period of 'railway mania', the boom years in Britain, when it was big business. The line from Leeds to Selby had been open for

An English railway station in 1838. (Euston Square)

barely five years. The fare would have cost them either 7/- first class or 4/6 second class, most likely the latter as they were on a tight budget. The Selby to York line wasn't opened until the following year, so a stagecoach journey followed. At York, they discovered that the coach to Driffield was full, so they were forced to take a slower fly. With the agreement of both the Nussey parents and Patrick Brontë, Henry had written and instructed John Hudson to pick up the women, so preventing them from taking lodgings at the waterfront. Hudson travelled to The Bell Hotel coach stop in Driffield to bear them off to his farm at Easton. But when they alighted at The Bell, he'd already returned home when the stagecoach had arrived without them. However, he had left firm instructions with the innkeeper that the pair should be brought to the farm by post chaise and it was by this mode of transport that the last stage of the tiring journey was completed. Luckily, the weather was fine and Charlotte and Ellen would have had a lovely view of the wooded wolds from the open chaise.

Their original plans thus thwarted, and very disappointed not to be nearer to the sea, Charlotte and Ellen decided to make the most of their month-long holiday.

It wasn't until the third day that Charlotte at last escaped with Ellen and walked eagerly towards the coast. From the top of Bessingby Hill she caught her first ever view of the sea, the broad and beautiful sweep of Bridlington Bay, with the chalk cliffs beyond. She was completely choked up with emotion. Sobbing quietly and unable to speak, she drank in the power and splendour of the German Ocean. She wanted to be left alone so Ellen thoughtfully walked ahead. Eventually, Charlotte rejoined her and Ellen was to recall many years later that her friend's eyes 'were red and swollen and she was trembling'. For the rest of that day, Ellen continued, Charlotte was 'quiet, subdued and exhausted.' They returned to the farm tired but elated after their secret walk and the Hudsons decided not to chide them.

Many happy days followed, and although the kindly Hudsons were at times over-protective, they did give the girls a fairly free rein. John Hudson was a true 'gentleman' farmer and his wife by all

A view of Bridlington in 1848 from Bessingby Hill, the point from which Charlotte first saw the sea. The Fire Station and Safeways now stand on the right.

This spreading horse chestnut tree at Easton marks the spot where the house stood in which Charlotte spent a very happy holiday.

accounts a 'sweet and kindly person.' The town had developed in two quite separate parts. Charlotte and Ellen explored Burlington at length (the delightfully preserved Old Town of today). *'Dugdale's Guide'* of the time describes it as 'a mile inland from Quay' and possessing 'a fine priory church and a number of handsome houses'. Quay, by the sea, was 'the resort of many noble and respectable families; having strong recommendations as a bathing-place, in the goodness of the shore, the cheapness and excellence of the provisions, and other accommodations; and the general liveliness of its appearance.'

In the fifth edition of *'Bridlington-Quay'*, published in 1877, Thomas Cape describes Bridlington as follows - 'The town has a clean and cheerful appearance, its streets are spacious, its various edifices of a respectable class....' and he continues '...the town is otherwise also indebted to nature, for its watering-place celebrity. The elements of air and water are possessed in their utmost purity;

and a combination of circumstances.... renders it unsurpassed and almost unequalled on these coasts, in the excellence of the sea-bathing'.

The two young women also took delight in wandering in the nearby autumnal countryside of fertile chalky wolds above the sea plain. They walked to nearby Thorpe Hall and Boynton Hall and to the village of Burton Agnes, where they visited a Mrs Brown and a Mrs Dalton with whom Henry Nussey had become friends during his time as a curate there. They also explored woods close by which Charlotte referred to as 'Harlequin Wood'. This is in fact 'Hallow Kiln' Wood, which the local farmhands still pronounce as 'allokin' Wood, so it is an excusable mistake. The wood is situated near the old Roman Road, now called Woldgate, which once ran to Stamford Bridge, and then on to York. Stories passed down by local farmers say that she was fascinated when she watched the washing of sheep in the Gypsey Race. The Race is a stream which runs through the valley in which the farmhouse stood.

1813. Sea bathing from huts on the north beach at Bridlington, from an engraving. Note the windmill and the old chalk lighthouse in the background.

It eventually flows into Clough (pronounced Clo) Hole in the harbour at Quay. Today, the practice of sheep washing would not be permitted in the Race, but it must have provided an an amusing spectacle for Charlotte in 1839.

There were other distractions too at Easton Farm. Mrs Hudson was the former Sophia Whipp, and her little niece, Fanny Whipp, was often to be found in the house. Charlotte, despite her awkwardness with children, became very fond of the engaging seven year old and calls her 'Little Hancheone', a German endearment. Fanny is most likely to have provided the character of Paulina Mary Home, the sweet child in Charlotte's third novel *'Villette'*, which is partly set in 'Bretton' based on the old town of Burlington. And in *'Shirley'*, her second published novel, the landlady of one of the curates has the name of Mrs Whipp. The farmhouse was two storied, partly chalk, partly brick, with a red tiled roof common in the area (the pantiles were made in Rudston or Beverley). In a watercolour which Charlotte painted during this first visit to the Hudsons (see front of book) a copy of which is in the Bayle Museum at the Priory, you can see that the house had a trellised porch, festooned with honeysuckle and ivy, and a pretty garden. She drew the Hudsons seated on a rustic garden bench with their dog beside them. Another portrait of Mrs Hudson which the talented artist Charlotte drew has been lost as have the pair of slippers she made.

The Hudsons stuck to a very rigid lifestyle, with rising times and mealtimes strictly adhered to. Bed-time was at nine thirty sharp. Charlotte longed to be nearer the sea, and later Ellen was to recall 'Whenever the sound of the sea reached her ears in the grounds around the house wherein she was captive*, her spirit longed to rush away and be close to it.' Desiring to be nearer the sea, the two begged their hosts to let them stay down at 'Quay' for the last week of their holiday. The Hudsons at last relented. They knew a Mrs Ann Booth who kept a lodging house in an area which is now Garrison Street, overlooking the sea just north of the harbour. And so it was arranged. Concerned about their being down amongst the fisherfolk, public houses and rough alleys, the Hudsons kept a close

---

* *Unlikely, as the house was more than 2 miles from the sea.*

eye on them, taking them fresh milk and provisions every day. The two young women revelled in this taste of freedom and found plenty to do, observing the gentry who took rooms for the fashionable 'season'. They watched the activities around the busy fishing harbour and on the sands where bathing huts proliferated. Ellen also wrote how Charlotte was particularly amused by the 'conventionality' of the swirling masses of people who marched in all their finery around and around on the small pier every evening.

She relates how the two joined the crowd on one occasion, but found it absurd to promenade in such a fashion, and retired to Sewerby cliffs to enjoy the tranquillity of the moonlight instead. She also describes how Charlotte was fascinated by the carryings on of the 'ranters' in a meeting house across the street from their lodgings. These primiitive Methodists made quite a racket and Charlotte, the daughter of a clergyman, was sorely tempted to join the congregation to see what on earth they were up to. But she refrained from doing so, telling Ellen that she believed they had a right to their own style of worship.

*The Regency seat from Easton farmhouse, on show
in the Bayle Museum in Bridlington.*

11

It was just as well that the Hudsons brought their gig down with food daily, as the meagre money the girls had with them barely paid the rent. Ellen Nussey writes in her book *'Reminiscences of CB by a 'Schoolfellow'*, 1871, '(they).. had desired to be their own providers, believing in their inexperience that they could do great things with the small sum of money they each had at their disposal, but at the end of the week when bills were asked for, they were thoroughly enlightened as to the propriety of the kind care which had guarded them - they discovered that modest appetites and moderate demands for attendance were of no avail as regarded the demands made upon their small finances. A week's experience sufficed to shew them the wisdom of not prolonging their stay, though the realisation of their *enjoyment* had been as intense as anticipation had depicted.' It is not recorded whether they tried the abundant fruits of the sea, but it is most likely they did. Few visit Bridlington today without partaking of a crab or two.

Unfortunately, the farmhouse at Easton was abruptly demolished in 1961 after it changed hands when the farm estate was sold by auction. This was supposedly due to its dilapidated state and, sadly, there had been no time to place a preservation order on it. Only a seat remains from the house, and this is to be found in the Bayle Museum near the Priory along with a reproduction of Charlotte's painting.

On returning home Charlotte realised that she had mislaid her spectacles, possibly in the excitement of packing to move to Mrs Booth's at 'Quay'. When she returned to Haworth she was quite lost without them, and wrote to Ellen to see if she could trace them - 'Did you chance, in your letter to Mr Hudson, to mention my spectacles? .....I can neither read, write, nor draw with comfort in their absence.....I do hope Madame won't refuse to give them up.'
So far as is known, they never turned up.

The Bridlington holiday left Charlotte refreshed and sparkling and its associations were to remain with her for the rest of her life. On 24th October that same year, still delighted by her memories, she wrote to Ellen, - 'Have you forgotten the sea by this time? Is it grown dim in your mind? Or can you still see it, - dark blue, and green, and foam-white; and hear it roaring roughly when the wind is high, or rushing softly when it is calm. I am as well as need be, and very fat. I think of Easton very often, and of worthy Mr Hudson, and his kind-hearted help-mate, and of our pleasant walks to Harlequin Wood, to Boynton, our merry evenings, our romps with little Hancheone, etc., etc. If we both live, this period of our lives will long be a theme of pleasant recollection...' Four days later, on 28 October, she wrote to Henry, still bubbling with her experiences - ' I enjoyed my late excursion with Ellen with the greater zest because such pleasures have not often chanced to fall in my way - I will not tell you what I thought of the sea, because I should fall into my besetting sin of enthusiasm.* I may, however, say that its glorious changes - its ebb and flow - the sound of its restless waves - formed a subject for contemplation that never wearied either the eye, the ear or the mind.'

A full year later, in the middle of a wuthering storm at Haworth, Charlotte still could not forget Bridlington ... 'from what quarter the wind blows, I cannot tell - but I should very much like to know how the great brewing-tub of Bridlington Bay works, and what sort of yeasty froth rises just now on the waves.'

§

The Sea Wall, much as it would have looked in 1839, with the Methodist Chapel perched near the edge of the cliff.

13

The term was used to mean excess or fanaticism in those days.

Walk 1
Easton, Old Town &
Bridlington Quay
4 miles, 2 hours - easy.

This walk begins on a road named Wold Gate, a mile past the tip and gypsy encampment. This old Roman road once led to Kilham and Stamford Bridge. Before that it was thought to be an important Neolithic trade route. In 1839 it was still called Fond Brigg Lane, referring to the old stone bridge under which a path from Carnaby passes. Wold Gate is to be found running due west out of Bridlington, parallel with the B1253 Scenic Route to York, where the A166 meets the A165. The simplest way to find it is to approach the hospital going up Bessingby Hill from town. Turn right at the lights, then take the next turning sharp left signposted to the town's waste disposal site. If you don't want to double the walking distance and time, I would recommend taking a taxi from town to the start point. (This costs around three pounds). The start point is two miles along Wold Gate at the first crossroads (where the road from Carnaby joins it.) Be sure to take note of Carnaby Temple* and also the wood which you pass on your left, a mile before the crossroads. This is Hallow Kiln Wood, in which Charlotte walked with Ellen. She mistakenly referred to it as 'Harlequin' Wood in her letters. At the crossroads turn right on a minor road and walk north through Sands Wood. Down the gentle slope is the vale where the road crosses the fenced Gypsey Race, a spot Charlotte loved. On your right is New Plantation.

The Race is a good sized stream which flows through the Great Wold Valley from its source near Wold Newton to Bridlington Harbour. The water comes from springs called 'gypsey' springs which ooze forth from the chalk wolds. They flow erratically when underground cavities are filled with rain. The name may come from wandering 'gypsies' or from 'gypsum' traces in the water, or from the greek 'gupos' meaning chalk. Or it could derive from

* *A residential folly built for its views in 1770 by Sir George Strickland of Boynton Hall.*

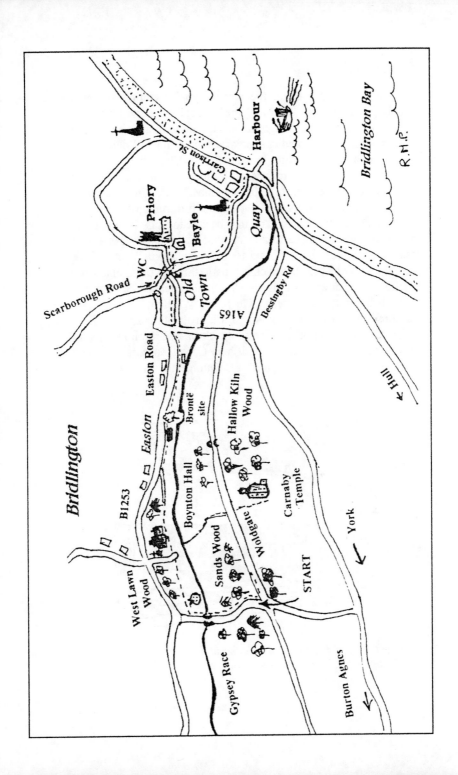

early norse settlers using the word 'gypa' meaning geyser, a bubbling waterspout. Anyway, the unpredictable and mysterious flow of the springs is thought to be supernatural, and an unusual flow is considered to predict a major calamity in the Wolds. It was very near here, in tranquil meadows, that Charlotte looked on, fascinated, as sheep were washed by local farmers in the Race, which would have been full in September. Continue on up the sloping road towards the B1253 road, but turn right just before you reach it, at a footpath sign. You may be able to pause here to pick a punnet or two of strawberries if you choose the right weeks in July! The wood which this path skirts is West Lawn Wood. Carry straight on along this broad chalky path through fields and across a stile, then down towards the church at Boynton. St Andrew's Church has a turkey lectern, celebrating William Strickland, the explorer, who lived in Boynton Hall in the late 1500's. He is believed to have introduced the first turkeys to Britain from North America, after an expedition with Jean Cabot sponsored by Henry VIII. Walk in through the gates of Boynton Hall (private) home to

One of the fine old bow fronted buildings in High Street in the Old Town of Bridlington. Others have been taken to the Castle Museum in York.

many generations of Stricklands, with its lovely Tudor brickwork. Queen Henrietta Maria (Charles I's wife) was once a guest here and 'borrowed' the family silver, but that's another story. Turn sharp left along a public footpath (once the main road). Walk through larch woods to a farm. Keeping a house and a caravan site on your right, continue until you re-encounter Easton Road.

Continue on the footpath towards Bridlington and the scattering of houses which is the hamlet of Easton. On your left is a white Georgian cottage (part of Easttfield Farm West) and almost directly opposite on the right hand side is the brick-walled entrance to Eastfield Farm East. This is where Charlotte and Ellen Nussey spent such a happy holiday in 1839. The farmhouse was demolished in 1961, but it stood just in front of the large green farm sheds, under the horse chestnut tree, where you can see a pile of rubble. In 1839 this road was an unsealed track. Linger, then walk to the end of the B1253 and, being very careful, cross the busy bypass (Well Lane) to the extension of Easton Road (no entrance for cars). The housing estate on your left has many Brontë associated names to its streets. The street you are on soon becomes Westgate, where wealthy merchants, doctors and solicitors built houses. Note the Avenues apartments, clearly dated 1714. Parts of

The High Street of Bridlington's Old Town in 1997.

17

Bridlington Priory as it is today.

Ye Olde Star Inn and No 6-7 date back to the 1600s. The latter, a redbrick building, now the Midland bank, belonged to the rich Hebblethwaite family. Its original windows are very rare. You are now in the High Street in the unspoilt Old Town of Bridlington which today is a conservation area and the best preserved mixture of old housing in Yorkshire. It still looks very much as it did when Charlotte visited and is thought to have been alluded to in her work. In a passage in the first paragraph of *'Villette'*, Lucy Snowe is in the town of 'Bretton' and looks out of the window of Mrs Bretton's house onto - 'a fine antique street, where Sundays and holidays seemed always to abide - so quiet was its atmosphere, so clean its pavement.' Later on, in Brussels, Lucy recalls Bretton. She pulls up a blind and looks out of a window, - 'half prepared to meet the calm, old, handsome buildings, and clean grey pavement of St Anne's Street, and to see at the end the towers of the minster.'

The Market Place to your left has been re-cobbled and street lamps add to the atmosphere. Pause to look at the stocks and the old K6 telephone box. Going on down High Street you will pass some lovely bow-fronted shops. No 64a, the chemist's shop, has had only three families running it in the past two hundred years and

18

boasts the original interior fittings and scales. Pop inside to have a look. No 64 next door, known as the Manor House, has stone blocks from the original priory incorporated into its structure, and opposite, No 67, once an ironmongers, has unusual brass rails to hold the glass in its bow front. Nos. 42-50 are amongst the oldest houses, hence their steep rooftops. No 43 was built in 1673, and the antique shop on your left once housed Burlington's third town hall on its first floor. There is a Dominican convent further along on the left. It dates from the early 1700s and has an 1825 Tuscan doorway.

No 16, Craven House, dates from the 1600s and had Francis Johnson, the well-known architect, as its resident until his death. William Kent, the architect who designed the interior of No 10 Downing Street, was born in the Old Town in 1684. At the end of the street relish the view of the Priory, then cross to the Bayle Museum, housed in what was the gatehouse (built in 1388) of the old Augustinian Priory. The Bayle is virtually all that remains intact after the dissolution of the monasteries, except for a small part of the church. If it is open, go into the Museum and take a look at the seat from Easton farmhouse and the copy of Charlotte's watercolour of the house. Also to be found on display in an upstairs room, is a pair of Queen Henrietta's elbow length gloves.

The Bayle Gate of the old Bridlington Priory.

19

The magnificent Priory Church, founded in 1113, is well worth exploring and is particularly noted for its wonderful windows. The Hudsons are buried in the graveyard and so is Fanny Whipp, whose married name was North. After a wander here you could, if you like, make a detour to No. 44 Scarborough Road, on the main road you have just crossed. The house is on the right going up towards the two roundabouts at the top of the slope. Standing outside the gate you will observe in a central first floor window a stained glass representation of Easton farmhouse, commissioned by a former resident, a farmer who moved into town in the 1950s.

*The stained glass window in the house in Scarborough
Road, which depicts Easton farmhouse.*

Walk eastwards straight down St John Street, Quay Road and Prospect Street into 'Quay'. At the end of Queen Street at the beginning of Prince Street, walk down to the harbour via Spring Pump Slipway (next to McDonalds). Here you will see a plaque commemorating the discovery of a fresh water spring in 1811. The cobble setts in the slipway helped horses to pull loads up the slope.

Turn left here and walk past Crane Wharf, where small boats are moored. Near here, at the beginning of the North Pier, is the spot where Charlotte watched the gentry parading in all their finery in 1839. Climb the circular steps behind you and directly in front of you is Garrison Street and the Esplanade which overlook Royal Princes Parade and the funfair. In 1839 this area was called the Sea Wall. The area in front is all reclaimed. Walk across the open paved area to the street. The house where Charlotte and Ellen stayed in lodgings with Mrs Booth was thought to be here in Garrison Street, but due to fires, serious wartime air raids and dereliction, nothing remains of the building. Nowadays all you will see are amusement arcades with flats above, although the view of the sea and cliffs is just as fine. The 'Ranters' Chapel which so amused Charlotte also stood near here, on the edge of the Sea Wall.

The old wooden pier at Bridlington Quay which was just about to be replaced with the present stone pier when Charlotte stayed in 1839.

In his book *'Bridlington-Quay'* Thomas Cape describes 'Quay', and the scene which Charlotte and Ellen would have seen from their window, as follows - 'It is situated on the verge of a beautiful bay of the sea, of which Flamborough Head, a bold promontory of chalk stone rock, forms a boundary on the one side, and the low land of the Holderness coast on the other.' He describes the beaches too .... 'hence, with a firm, gently-sloping, sandy beach, pure water, and comparative immunity from danger, bathing, which is generally considered merely a healthy and pleasant recreation, may be indulged in here as a perfect luxury.' On the subject of the harbour, he says, - 'the pier .... is an efficient and attractive promenade, with a full view of the bay and surrounding coast, and of the waves breaking in white, fringe-like foam, over the Smithwick Sands in the distance.'

Finish your walk with a well deserved cup of coffee and an ice in Jerome's Restaurant, which is a little further along in the midst of the funfair, on the sea side next to the old Floral Hall.

§

The Sea Wall in Bridlington as it looked in 1895.

22

Walk 2
Sewerby, Danes Dyke, Flamborough Village
6 miles, 3 hours - medium grade (steps)

This walk, which Charlotte and Ellen almost certainly did, covers a short section of the 20 mile long Headland Way. It begins on the north beach side of Bridlington, at the Expanse Hotel on North Marine Promenade. Set off in a northerly direction up the gentle slope from the train stop where the little people-mover train begins its route to Sewerby Hall in summertime. You will pass a modern convalescent home on your left. Near here is the spot where Charlotte and Ellen Nussey sat in the moonlight in September 1839 after they had fled the fashionable masses promenading on the pier. One can imagine how they felt. On a clear evening this must be one of the loveliest views on the Yorkshire coast, with the white cliffs of Flamborough Head to the north, and Spurn point to the south. Walk along the cliff path to Sewerby Hall and you will find the delightful cricket ground perched on the cliff with a ha-ha* behind it. You may even have a chance to pass time watching a laid-back local match. Home to the Greame family for 200 years, Sewerby Hall, set in 50 glorious acres of gardens, was built in 1715. A road once passed in front of it. Yarborough Greame added the conservatory (orangery) in 1856 to grow his exotic fruit, and it has recently been lovingly restored. The museum and gardens are well worth a visit. The Hall houses the Amy Johnson* collection, an art gallery and local achaeological, historical and environmental exhibits.

Carry on along the cliff path (taking care, it can be dangerous) to where Danes Dyke earthworks meets the sea. You will have to descend and ascend steps here. The Danes did settle here, but the Dyke was dug as a defence much earlier, by Iron Age settlers 3000 years ago (the Parisi). Continue to South Landing, which is a good spot to pause for a paddle.

23

* *ha-ha - a sunk fence bounding park.*
* *Amy Johnson - the famous aviatrix.*

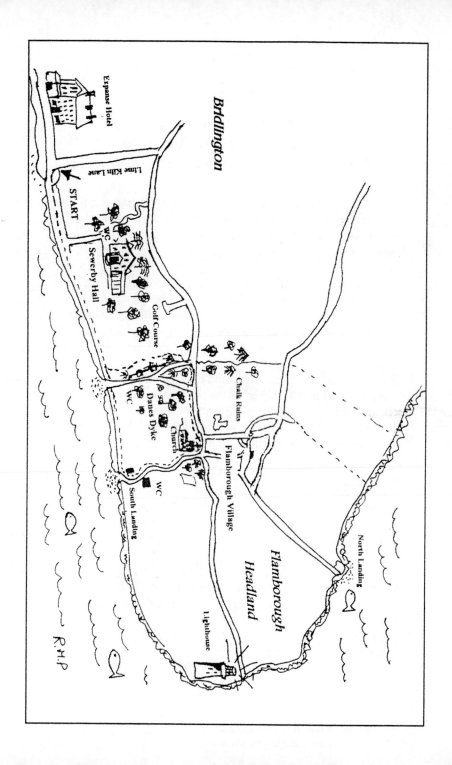

The new lifeboat station is situated here and fishing cobles also land their catches. This was always the alternative fishing base to North Landing, depending on the wind and tides. There was a port here in medieval times and a pier in the 1400s. At very low tide you may catch a glimpse of the old stones from the ancient pier base. There are many smooth stones on the beach with holes in the middle. This is caused by minute boring creatures called piddicks. Turn inland here and walk up the hill to the Heritage Coast Information Centre where you will find a good picnic area, toilets and information on all aspects of this protected coastal area.

Continue to walk inland along the only road, which will bring you to Flamborough village, once known for smuggling. The name comes from 'flaen', an arrow point, which is the shape of the headland. Local men, until the nineteen-fifties, were lowered over the high cliffs around here to gather gulls' eggs (particularly those of guillemots) to sell. These men were known locally as 'climmers'.

'Climmers' carrying out their hair-raising task of gathering birds' eggs by swinging over the cliff edge on ropes.

Continue to walk inland along the only road, South Sea Road, which will bring you to Flamborough village. You could take a detour here and explore what is still essentially a fishing village. Simple whitewashed cottages with crab pots in their gardens leave you in no doubt of this. The locals are gruff but friendly and it's worth popping into one of the numerous pubs to try to eavesdrop on what's left of the unusual local dialect, which emerged from Danish origins. If you're short of time, turn left at the junction of South Sea Road with Lighthouse Road (a playing field is on your right). At the next junction (100 yards) in a field in front of you, you will see all that remains of the Constable family's old manor house. These are the blocks from the base of the chalk tower.

Turn left and follow the curve of the road to St Oswald's Church, taking note of the fish vane on the steeple. St Oswald is the patron saint of seamen north of the Humber. Do go inside if you have time. There has been a church on the site since 1150 and its notable features include a beautifully carved medieval rood screen and loft and an unusual Norman font and chancel. The Strickland Pardon, a replica from 1660, is fascinating and so is the Flamborough Book of Service, with its illustrated panels naming all those engaged in War service. There is also an interesting Squint behind the altar. The strangest thing in the church to my mind is the Constable Tomb, a memorial to Sir Marmaduke who died in 1530. On top of it is the upper half of a skeleton and inside the ribcage is a heart and a lump thought to be a toad. Sir Marmaduke, of Flodden Field fame, is supposed to have died after swallowing a toad which ate his heart out! In the Vestry you will find another unusual item. A pair of framed white paper gloves hang on the wall. These were a local custom and were last used at the funeral of a Miss Major in 1761. When a maiden died, the coffin was carried by women and the procession was always led by a girl carrying a pair of white paper gloves.

Continue on the road towards Bridlington, past an old pump on your left, and soon after going up a hill, you'll find the Danes Dyke exit for cars. Ignore this and enter instead by the entrance in a dip a quarter mile further along on your left. Enter this road and turn down steps and a path which you will see almost immediately on your right. Now you will find yourself on a lovely walk through woodland beside the Dyke. Many birds are to be found in this beauty spot. Head towards the sea and you will soon pass over a wooden bridge. Continue up the slope and where the path branches at the top choose the one which leads into the open along the edge of the golf course rather than that which follows the right side of the Dyke. This will save you having to climb the steep path up from the beach. Turn right at the signpost on the clifftop and carry on towards Sewerby. On a clear day the view of Bridlington and Spurn Point is superb from here. Retrace your steps to the Expanse Hotel in Bridlington.

§

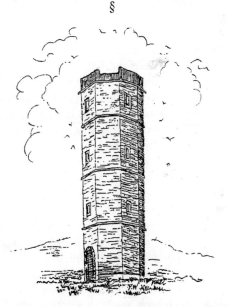

The old chalk lighthouse, erected in 1674, which still stands at North Landing in Flamborough. Lovingly restored in 1996 with an English Heritage grant, it was originally used as a lookout and fires were lit on top of the tower to enable ships to avoid the treacherous headland in stormy weather.

Chapter 2
Anne in Scarborough, 1841-45

All three Brontë sisters at various times attempted to earn their livings as teachers or governesses during the ten years between 1835 and 1845. They were educated to a much higher degree than those less fortunate beings who worked in the mills in Haworth but, even with their father employed as perpetual curate, the family's income was not substantial and it was important that the unmarried young women should gain employment. Their intermittent teaching experiences certainly proved valuable, in a literary sense, as both Charlotte and Anne subsequently wrote novels about governesses - *'Jane Eyre'* and *'Agnes Grey'.*

However, it was only the quieter, more stoic Anne who managed to stick the profession. In 1840 she took on a post as governess to the Robinson children at the Reverend Edmund Robinson's family home at Thorp Green Hall, at Little Ouseburn near York. At first the twenty year old was desperately homesick, never having been so far from home before, and she wrote heartbreaking letters home saying how much she disliked her position. But she was to show an endurance for the work that her sisters lacked and she remained with the Robinsons for five years. During this time the Robinson family spent a good part of every summer in spacious lodgings in Scarborough, and Anne accompanied them. In her diary of 1841 she records her first sighting of the sea, two years after Charlotte had done so at Bridlington. She was not too keen on the position of governess and it was around this time that she and Charlotte entertained the idea of opening a private school of their own, possibly on the Yorkshire coast. Aunt Branwell promised to advance them some money towards it. Charlotte wrote to Ellen Nussey in 1841 - 'In thinking of all possible places ....where we could establish a school, I have thought of Burlington (Bridlington)....there are a hundred reasons why it should be an impracticable one...it is far from home, etc. Still, I fancy the ground in the East Riding is less fully occupied than in the West .I fear much time will elapse before any plan is executed.' Some years later, the three sisters decided that the school should be in Haworth. They designed a one page advertisement, but nothing ever came of the plan, although it did bear fruit in one sense. The 'school' project was the reason that Emily and Charlotte later went to the Pensionnat Heger in Brussels to improve their French and German. And Charlotte subsequently wrote *'The Professor'* and *'Villette'* as a result of her experiences.

Scarborough, with its long history as a spa town (there are natural springs under the cliffs) was at this time a very fashionable resort, sometimes referred to as 'North East England's Bay of Naples'. Grand houses with sea views lined the terraces and crescents and many had been recently built as dedicated lodging houses, with self-contained facilities and housekeepers for each apartment. It was in the new and very smart Wood's Lodgings, on what is now St Nicholas Cliff, that Anne stayed with the Robinsons. The style was Italianate, and from the cliff side you could see its balustrades and pilasters. The Grand Hotel stands on the site today.

During these summers Anne grew to love Scarborough, with its theatres and galleries and the lively events laid on for the summer season. There was another side to the town too - the fishing folk and winding streets of the older harbour area, and Anne's curiosity sometimes led her into these streets. She adored the beach, the castle, and the sea. After Haworth's smoke and grime (although it did have its redeeming moors) it must have been heavenly to be at the seaside. Anne's first novel *'Agnes Grey'*, published in 1847 and written in the first person, is the tale of Agnes Grey, a governess who sets up a school, much of it based on her own experiences of Scarborough. Within it is a description of a seaside town 'A-', which Agnes refers to as 'the fashionable watering-place'.

Anne's love of the sea is clear in *'Agnes Grey'*. The heroine states...'I would often gladly pierce the town to obtain the pleasure of a walk beside it (the sea) whether with the pupils, or alone with my mother during the vacations. It was delightful to me at all times and seasons'.

In Chapter 24 the young governess describes an early morning stroll on the beach.

...'I was dressed and out when the church clock struck a quarter to six. There was a feeling of freshness and vigour in the very streets; and when I got free of the town, when my foot was on the sands and my face towards the broad, bright bay, no language can describe the effect of the deep, clear azure of the sky and the ocean, the bright morning sunshine on the semi-circular barrier of craggy cliffs surmounted by green swelling hills, and on the smooth, wide sands, and the low rocks out at sea - looking, with their clothing of weeds and moss, like little grass-grown islands - and above all, on the brilliant, sparkling waves. And then, the unspeakable purity and freshness of the air!....there was just enough heat to enhance the value of the breeze, and just enough wind to keep the whole sea in motion, to make the waves come bounding to the shore, foaming and sparkling, as if wild with glee...My footsteps were the first to press the firm unbroken sands; - nothing before had trampled them since last night's flowing tide had obliterated the deepest marks of yesterday, and left it fair and even, except where the subsiding water had left behind it the traces of dimpled pools and little running streams. Refreshed, delighted, invigorated, I walked along, forgetting all my cares, feeling as if I had wings on my feet, and could go at least forty miles without fatigue, and experiencing a sense of exhileration to which I had been an entire stranger since the early days of my youth.'

In Chapter 25 she also describes a scene which is obviously Castle Hill in Scarborough. Mr Weston tells Agnes that he wants to take her for a walk that evening to ... 'a bold hill on the land side, and towards the sea a steep precipice, from the summit of which a glorious view is to be had'. And this is where he proposes to her after they romantically watch a brilliant sunset. Also in Chapter 25 of 'Agnes Grey' St Mary's Parish Church is used in the narrative. The couple approach it from the town on the same walk, after a rainstorm.... 'we came in sight of the venerable old church, and the hill, with the deep blue sea beyond it'.

Anne's second novel, 'The Tenant of Wildfell Hall', published in 1848, relates the tale of a woman married to a drunken rake.

Her experiences with her infamous brother Branwell provided the raw material. In the novel, Anne has not forgotten the Yorkshire coast when she paints a verbal picture of the area around Wildfell Hall. In Chapters 5 and 6 the geographical descriptions of the countryside as it changes nearer to the sea are very like the terrain of the North Yorkshire Moors which are situated just inland from Scarborough.

It is most likely, although not widely documented, that Branwell also visited Scarborough. In 1843 he was working as a booking clerk at Luddenden Foot on the Leeds and Manchester Railway. On Anne's recommendation, in January, the classically-educated Branwell took on a post as gentleman-tutor to young Edmund Robinson at Thorp Green Hall. Anne was less miserable and lonely with him around, although, as a compulsive liar and boaster, he often proved to be an embarrassment. He went with the family to Scarborough during at least one of the summers he was in their employ. But Anne was to suddenly leave the family in June 1845 and a month later, Branwell was dismissed after a foolish episode where he claims to have fallen in love with Mrs Robinson, and to have received her encouragement.

§

Scarborough as it looked in the mid 1800's when Anne Brontë stayed. The building on the right is Wood's lodgings.

31

Chapter 3
Scarborough, Filey, Bridlington
Anne's Death, May 1849

It shouldn't be forgotten that, without Anne's perseverance as a governess and wage earner, it would have been impossible for her two sisters to have travelled to Brussels to study at the Pensionnat Heger during 1842 and 1843. In January 1842, Charlotte and Emily crossed the Channel to gain language qualifications in order to one day open their dreamt-of school in Yorkshire. The death of Aunt Branwell cut their first year short and only Charlotte, driven by a desire for self-development, returned to Brussels for what turned out to be an unhappy year, when she became infatuated with M. Constantin Heger, a married man. She said she had gone 'longing for wings, to know, to learn, for wealth', but in that year - 'her wings drooped'. She returned in January 1844. By the autumn of 1845, with Anne finished at Thorp Green, all three sisters were back in Haworth and the serious novel writing had begun. In 1847 they published their best known novels to much acclaim.* All three novels were published under pseudonyms, 'Currer Bell', (Charlotte), 'Ellis Bell' (Emily), and 'Acton Bell' (Anne). Anne's second novel *The Tenant of Wildfell Hall'*, published in the summer of 1848, was at the time a failure.

In September 1848, Branwell Brontë died at the age of thirty-one. After suffering the disgrace of dismissal by the Robinsons, he had held down various undemanding jobs. But increasingly he spent much of his time in public houses. He was both self-indulgent and big-headed. When he began over-indulging in brandy and opium his health declined rapidly. By the end he was out of control, ranting at night and lying in a stupor by day. His father remained devoted to his son, despite his despair over his behaviour. The family had had much to endure since he returned to live at the parsonage, but they hadn't realised quite how much damage he had done to himself.

32

* *'Jane Eyre', 'Wuthering Heights'* and *'Agnes Grey'*.

He spent only one day in bed before he died in his father's arms on a Sunday evening in the upstairs bedroom. Charlotte hadn't believed he was ill and, being less pious than her sisters, his death came as a terrible shock to her. She took to her bed for a week after the deathbed scene, with migraines and sickness. While they must have been relieved to be free of his problematic presence, the three sisters mourned for a beloved brother who had once shown such promise. But worse was to come. Emily caught a cold at Branwell's funeral and ten weeks later, on December 19th 1848, she too was dead, aged just 30, from consumption. It is said that her psychological state - she was always a loner - and her absolute refusal of any medication contributed to her death. She'd ignored all symptoms, even tottering out to feed her beloved dogs on the day of her death, and died heroically on the dining room couch. Charlotte was to write to Ellen later of her sister's nightmare 'death-day'... 'it was very terrible, she was torn conscious, panting, reluctant though resolute out of a happy life.'

Two Brontës now lay in Haworth Church and yet, a month later, Anne was sickening before the family's eyes. Her decline was gradual, unlike Emily's sudden demise, but she had suffered colds and asthma for a long time. In early winter 1848 she was soaked in a rainstorm on the 4 mile walk to Keighley on her and Charlotte's way to a publisher's appointment in London. In January 1849 she was diagnosed to be suffering from consumption in both lungs - a virtual death sentence. She subsequently underwent many treatments, desperately wanting to live. Her poems written in these last weeks reveal a feeling of unfulfilled ambition. Charlotte, in despair, wrote to W. Smith Williams, the reader at her publisher, round this time...'Too often I feel like one crossing an abyss on a narrow plank - a glance around might quite unnerve...' At this time, April, Anne convinced herself that sea air would do her good, although she knew in her heart she was dying, and she begged for a visit to Scarborough. Charlotte vigorously opposed the idea, probably from fear of hastening her death. Anne's specialist, a Dr.Teale from Leeds, eventually agreed to the plan, more from mercy than hope. Anne had money from a legacy to pay for the trip. It was decided to grant her wishes and when the weather improved in May, for both Charlotte and Ellen Nussey to accompany Anne to the coast.

Charlotte wrote to Ellen on 16th May 'It is with a heavy heart that I prepare - and earnestly do I wish that the fatigue of the journey were well over - it may be borne better than I expect - but when I see the daily increasing weakness - I know not what to think. I fear you will be shocked when you see Anne - but be on your guard not to express your feelings - indeed I can trust both your self-possession and your kindness.' Charlotte also wrote elsewhere at the time....'Ellen Nussey accompanies us at her own kind and friendly wish. I would not refuse her society but I dared not urge her to go, for I have little hope that the excursion will be one of pleasure or benefit to those engaged in it. Anne is extremely weak. She herself has a fixed impression that the sea-air will give her the chance of regaining strength - that chance therefore she must have.'

And so the two Brontës returned to their beloved Yorkshire Coast. The sisters had arranged to meet Ellen at Leeds Station on Wednesday 23rd May but they were delayed and Ellen was left waiting on the platform. Before making the decision to travel to Haworth to join them, she had to watch two coffins taken off trains. The three finally left on the Thursday. Patrick Brontë and Tabby and Martha, the faithful servants, knew that they would never see Anne again as they bade her farewell. By now she was emaciated and could hardly walk.

York Minster.

The Grand Hotel, Scarborough, built in 1867, which today stands on the site of No 2. The Cliff, where Anne Brontë died.

But they were resigned and, like Charlotte, wanted Anne to die where she was happiest. This last trip of Anne's was typical of her pious striving for dignity. She was, like the character Agnes in her book *'Agnes Grey'*, -'tranquil and undismayed'.

The three women travelled by coach from Keighley to Leeds, then caught the train from Leeds to York, where they stayed that night. They booked in at the George Hotel in Whip-ma-Whop-ma-Gate, and, after happily shopping for bonnets, Anne was taken in a bath-chair to visit the splendid York Minster, which she had seen before with the Robinsons. When they reached Scarborough by train on Friday (the railway line had been opened in 1846) Charlotte had decided in advance to take rooms in a lodging house even though Miss Wooler, her old teacher and friend, had rented a house in Scarborough for the season and offered them rooms. Perhaps she wished to spare her the pain, and she knew Anne longed to be near the sea. Their lodgings, which cost 30 shillings a week, were at No 2. The Cliff, very near Wood's Lodgings by Cliff Bridge where Anne had stayed with the Robinsons in happier circumstances. The room had a splendid view of the bay, the harbour and the castle.

35

The following day, Saturday, Anne took a brief walk in the morning which exhausted her, but she was well enough in the afternoon to take a ride in a donkey carriage along the sands. It is recorded by Ellen Nussey that Anne even took hold of the reins herself for fear that the driver would push the donkey too hard.

On Sunday, 27th May, Charlotte wrote again to W. Smith Williams, the reader at her publisher in London, '...As Anne sits at the window she can look down at the sea, which this morning is as calm as glass. She says if she could breathe more freely she would be comfortable at this moment, but she cannot breathe freely.' It was decided Anne was too unwell to attend church that morning but in the afternoon she walked down to the beach and rested on a seat while Charlotte and Ellen strolled a little further.

St Nicholas Cliff as it looked when Charlotte, Anne and Ellen stayed in 1849 prior to Anne's death.

A stunning sunset lit the sea that evening as they watched from the sitting room. Anne had been pulled to the window in her easy chair and Ellen wrote later... 'her face became illumined almost as much as the glorious scene she gazed upon. Little was said, for it was plain that her thoughts were driven by the imposing view before her to penetrate forwards to the regions of unfading glory'.

Next morning, Monday 28th May, Anne had dressed herself by 7 a.m. She was carried downstairs for breakfast but grew weaker as the day passed, and it became clear she was dying. When she faded away at 2 o'clock she was resigned and placid, and had just spoken to Charlotte, saying 'take courage'. The death was so calm that later that day the landlady, quite unaware of happenings, put her head round the door to say that dinner was served. Charlotte decided that Anne should be buried at Scarborough, to save her father the distress of another family funeral. She felt he would not be able to bear Anne's coffin arriving at his door.

Anne's gravestone in St Mary's Churchyard, Scarborough.

37

On Wednesday 30th May Anne was buried in the graveyard of St Mary's Church on Castle Hill which overlooks South Bay. St Mary's was being restored, so the service took place in Christ Church in Vernon Road instead. This church, which was next to the present library, no longer stands. The funeral was attended only by Charlotte, Ellen Nussey and probably, Miss Wooler.

Charlotte wrote to her father to tell him of events and he wrote back, urging her to stay on at the coast for a while. The distraught Charlotte hardly knew which way to turn. In a letter written to Smith Williams she wrote ..'I cannot rest here, but neither can I go home....I shall wander a week or two on the East Coast, and only stay at quiet, lonely places.' In the event, the two stayed a further three weeks. Ellen was impatient to visit the Hudsons at Easton Farm in Bridlington, but Charlotte wanted to rest. They stayed for a week in Filey, at a Mrs Smith's lodgings called Cliff House in what is now Belle Vue Street. In those days it had a sea view. The house, which bears a plaque, still stands today. It now houses a cafe, 'The Brontë Vinery'. Mrs Smith, their land-lady,

The Parish Church of St. Mary, Castle Hill, Scarborough.

38

didn't realise who her famous visitor was and, regrettably, she threw out the letters which Charlotte wrote on her return home. On 13th June Charlotte wrote from Filey to Smith Williams again, '...Filey, where we have been for the last week...is a small place with a wild rocky coast - its sea is very blue - its cliffs are very white - its sands very solitary - it suits Ellen and myself better than Scarborough which is too gay.' Later in the letter, she described the depths of her feelings as the oldest and remaining child of the family - 'A year ago, - had a prophet warned me how I should stand in June 1849 - how stripped and bereaved - had he foretold the autumn, the winter, the spring of suffering to be gone through - I should have thought - this can never be endured. It is over. Branwell - Emily - Anne, are gone like dreams - gone as Maria and Elizabeth (her younger sisters) were twenty years ago. One by one I have watched them fall asleep on my arm - and closed their glazed eyes - I have seen them buried one by one...'

Filey, although smaller than Scarborough, was already a resort but retained its character as a fishing village with traditional east coast fishing cobles (boats). The town was just seeing its first real development, some fine terraced houses, built from 1840 onwards. There had been a famous chalybeate 'spaw well' on the top of Carr Naze, but by then it had dried up. Filey Brigg which juts out into the sea, is impressive. Charlotte would also have admired the view of the chalk cliffs of Bempton to the south, spectacular in clear weather.

After a week at Filey, Charlotte and Ellen travelled to the Hudsons at Easton Farm in Bridlington, their first visit since that happy autumn of 1839. Charlotte had a deadline for her novel *'Shirley'*, and spent much of her time there writing and reading in the garden. She had brought the manuscript with her and Mrs Gaskell, Charlotte's first biographer, maintained that Chapter 24 was written in the summerhouse at Easton. Called *'The Valley of the Shadow of Death'*, it is a very emotional portrait. The chapter tells how the heroine, Caroline Helstone, recovers from a life-threatening illness.

Charlotte caught a heavy cold during the stay at Easton. Terrified that she may be sickening with Anne's illness, she visited a High Street doctor in his Quay surgery for medication. On top of this, she was already worrying about what Haworth would be like. Writing to Smith Williams from Easton she said, 'I intend to return home to Papa. May I retain strength and cheerfulness enough to be a comfort to him and to bear up against the weight of the solitary life to come - it will be solitary - I cannot help dreading the very experience of it'.

She eventually returned home on 20th June, arriving at the Haworth parsonage in the evening. Charlotte described the moving scene in a letter to Ellen written on 23rd June.....'I got here a little before eight o'clock. All was clean and bright waiting for me. Papa and the servants were well; and all received me with an affection which should have consoled. The dogs* seemed in strange ecstasy. I am certain they regarded me as the harbinger of others. The dumb creatures thought as I was returned, those who had been so

Cliff House at Filey, which can be found in Belle Vue Street.

40

*Keeper, Emily's devoted dog and Flossie, Anne's beloved spaniel, continued to look for their mistresses, breaking Charlotte's heart afresh.

long absent were not far behind. I left Papa soon and went into the dining room: I shut the door - I tried to be glad that I was come home. I have always been glad before...but this time joy was not to be the sensation. I felt that the house was all silent - the rooms were all empty - I remembered where the three were laid - in what dark narrow dwellings - never more to reappear on earth. So the sensation of desolation and bitterness took possession of me. The agony that was to be undergone, and was not to be avoided, came on - I underwent it, & passed a dreary evening and night; and a mournful morrow - to-day I am better. I do not know how life will pass but I certainly do feel confident in Him who has upheld me hitherto'. In the same letter she added ... 'The great trial is when evening closes and night approaches - At that hour we used to assemble in the dining room - we used to talk - Now I sit by myself - necessarily I am silent. I cannot help thinking of their last days, remembering their affliction - perhaps this will become less poignant in time. Let me thank you once more, dear Ellen, for your kindness to me, which I do not mean to forget'.

After the devastation of losing three of her loved ones in nine months, Charlotte somehow returned to work that autumn on '*Shirley*' which had been started in 1847. She wrote bravely to Smith Williams... 'Labour must be the cure, not sympathy - Labour is the only radical cure for rooted sorrow...my work is my best companion - hereafter I look for no great earthly comfort except what congenial occupation can give.' Charlotte worked obsessively through the summer and by the end of August, she had completed the novel. '*Shirley*' was published on 26th October 1849. The story, with its industrial background of the rebellion of the Luddite cloth-dressers against machinery, was not as successful as '*Jane Eyre*' but is still a notable work. The task of writing it helped Charlotte to put her sadness from her mind for short periods at least. Later she was to reflect... 'It took me out of the dark and desolate reality into an unreal but happier region'.

It was around this time that Charlotte's name began to be widely linked with that of 'Currer Bell'. The secret was out at last.

§

Walk 3
Scarborough Beach, Castle, Anne's Grave, St Mary's Church
2 miles, 1½ hours - Medium steep

Start this walk at St Nicholas Cliff, the crescent in front of the Grand Hotel in Scarborough, high above the beach. On the front wall of the hotel you will a blue plaque declaring that Anne died on this site. You will also see the impressive iron bridge, Cliff Bridge, to the south of the hotel, which was relatively new when the Brontës came to Scarborough. It was built by Outhett in 1827 to give easier access to the Spa when the Cliff Bridge Company took over the Spa from the Corporation. There used to be a toll to pay to cross it. From the windows of Wood's Lodgings and The Cliff, Branwell, the two sisters and Ellen Nussey, who all stayed here, would have had a good view. In the summer many bathing huts could be seen. Sea bathing had been popular since the 1700s and before Victorian times it had been common for men to go out in local cobles (small fishing boats) and jump into the sea naked, or even bathe naked from the beach.

St Nicholas Cliff, Scarborough, with Cliff Bridge in the background.

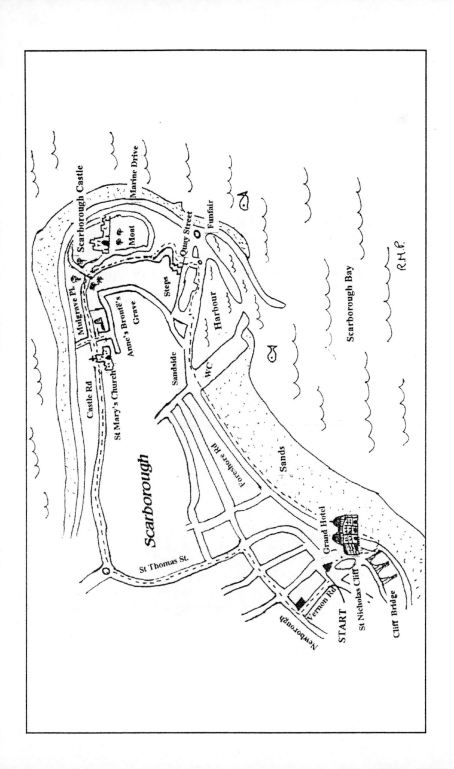

By the mid 1800s, however, everyone used bathing huts, many of them on wheels. These were drawn into the sea (often by horses) for added privacy. Further along the beach to the south you will see the Spa, where the spring waters were taken in various forms. Charlotte and Anne both bathed discreetly in Scarborough during their visits.

Both Scarborough and Bridlington owed their popularity to their reputation as Spa towns (until 1826 spelt Spaw). Visitors flocked to partake of the healthy, healing waters. Scarborough's natural bubbling cliff springs, which were discovered in 1620 by a Mrs Farrer, were 'chalybeate' (pronounced kal-lib-be-it) springs, i.e. containing iron salts. The magnesium sulphate also contained in the waters was as healthy as Andrews' Liver Salts and they were supposed to be superior to the waters in Bath. The first cistern for the waters was built in 1698 and later far grander buildings were erected on the site of the spring. The present building was started in 1877 and the council took it over in 1957.

The plaque on the Grand Hotel in Scarborough which states that Anne died in a house on this site in May, 1849.

44

The view of the harbour and Scarborough Castle which Anne Brontë would have had from the window of her summer lodgings.

Don't cross Cliff Bridge. Instead, walk down the path to the left of it under the funicular to the sands below. This is the beach across which Anne was transported in the donkey cart just before her death. Carry on along the beach northward towards the harbour and castle. There was no promenade here in the Brontës' time. Head for the harbour, which has three piers and dates from 1225 when Henry III granted 40 oaks from his woods to begin building. Look for Richard III's house on the opposite side, which bears a plaque. He supposedly stayed here in 1483, but the present building is of a much later date. It now houses a restaurant and coffee lounge. Cross the road and continue along Sandside until you find Quay Street on the left by the Ivy House Cafe (near a flagstaff in a bricked circle). Walk 100 yards up Quay Street and look for the Salmon Steps ahead of you. To the right are some quaint old buildings. Walk up Salmon Steps and turn right then sharp left where you see the steps signposted to the castle. (Don't take the sealed path which runs parallel to its left). Pause often as you climb for lovely views of the south bay which can be enjoyed from here. Higher up you will follow the moat of the castle on your right until three paths converge. Climb the middle steps to the Castle entrance.

Scarborough Castle's Barbican Gate is one of the best examples of such an edifice in the country. If you have time, a tour is a must, and it will also include the Roman Signal Station on the hill. The Castle was built in the 12th century by William le Gros, Earl of Albemarle, who led the Yorkshire Barons at the Battle of the Standards near Northallerton in 1138. King John came here in the 1200s and King Richard III and his Queen came in 1484. The Castle underwent many sieges and, in the Civil War, Scarborough was the only Royalist port on the East Coast. But in 1645 the garrison surrendered to Parliament. In 1914 The German fleet bombarded the Castle and town, and part of the Castle was damaged, including the barracks which Anne Brontë would have seen on her many strolls up the hill. You will see the superb view from here which is one she really loved and which she described in *'Agnes Grey'*. In Chapter 25 of the novel, Mr Weston tells Agnes that he wants to take her for a walk that evening to ... 'a bold hill on the land side, and towards the sea a steep precipice, from the summit of which a glorious view is to be had'. And this is where Mr Weston proposes to Agnes after they watch a vivid sunset.

After your Castle exploration, continue down the road (Castle Road) which takes you from the castle entrance towards the Parish Church of St. Mary. This too is described in Chapter 25 of *'Agnes Grey'*, but the couple are approaching from the other direction .... 'we came in sight of the venerable old church, and the hill, with the deep blue sea beyond it'. To your left at the small crossroads you will see an iron gate at the top of Church Lane which is the entrance to the walled graveyard. Enter and directly in front of you is Anne Brontë's well-tended and planted grave, with a seat placed conveniently for contemplation. Note that her age is wrongly engraved - it should read 29. When you are ready, exit the graveyard, turn right and make a small detour up the small road opposite (Mulgrave Place) for a superb view of the North Bay. Retrace your steps and explore the church if you have time. It is 12th Century and belonged to the Bridlington Augustinian Priory for some time. Various parts have been rebuilt over the centuries and the west front is the oldest . The present tower dates from 1669.

Carry on down Castle Road keeping the church on your left and look out for Wilson's Mariners' Asylum built in 1836, which Anne would have seen. Turn left at the roundabout down busy St. Thomas Street and walk its length. About halfway along on the left there was once a theatre which Anne attended with the Robinsons. When you reach the lights at the end you will see the pedestrianised Newborough on your right - today the main shopping street of Scarborough. A huge library once stood here which Anne would definitely have used. Walk up Newborough past two interesting lanes on your left, and then you will come to Vernon Road on the same side. Turn into this street. Here on the left stood the long ago demolished Christ Church in which Anne's funeral service was held, attended by Charlotte, Ellen Nussey and Miss Wooler. Today, Christ Church House stands in its place. Walk to the end of Vernon Road, turn left and you will find yourself back at St Nicholas Cliff. A well-deserved cup of coffee can be found in any number of nice tea shops in this area.

§

Fishing activities in an east coast fishing town.

47

Walk 4
Speeton Village and Beach
3 miles, 2½ hours - VERY steep - rewarding.

Speeton is a small village to the north of Bridlington, smack on the East/North Yorkshire border. You'll find the road to the village off the B1229 road. Look out for the signpost on the right, approximately 1½ miles after Bempton and Buckton villages. As you go towards Speeton, note Buckton Hall about a mile after Bempton on your right. This large house was built in 1745 but was gutted by fire in 1919. You can't miss Speeton, its main landmark being the old coastguard station and cottages on the highest point on this part of the coast. A windmill once stood near here and some of the village houses have the bricks from it incorporated into their structure. There are two hills, one called Beacon Hill, and the other, according to Thomas Cape in his 1877 book, '*Bridlington-Quay*', was called 'Bonne fire Hill'. During Speeton's early history, invasions by Barbarians were common and this elevated spot was ideal as a lookout from which the alarm could be raised to those inland. Speeton probably derived its name from the Saxon *spyrion* or *spyrizean,* to 'look out, or watch', an obvious choice.

Carry on through the village and turn left at the duckpond and you will see ahead of you, just as Charlotte once did, the charming little St Leonard's church which is built of stone and some chalk. It has an unusual pagoda shaped tower and the bell is a ship's bell. The church was used to store brandy and rum in smuggling days. In the field next door a flock of sheep grazes - English Leicester longwools - one of the oldest flocks in the UK, which have been with the same family since 1834. Perhaps Charlotte saw their woolly ancestors? It is said that the north wall is preserved from the weather by sheltering sheep, who leave lanolin on the stones! The church is thought to be Saxon, restored by the Normans and it was once part of Bridlington Priory's estate.

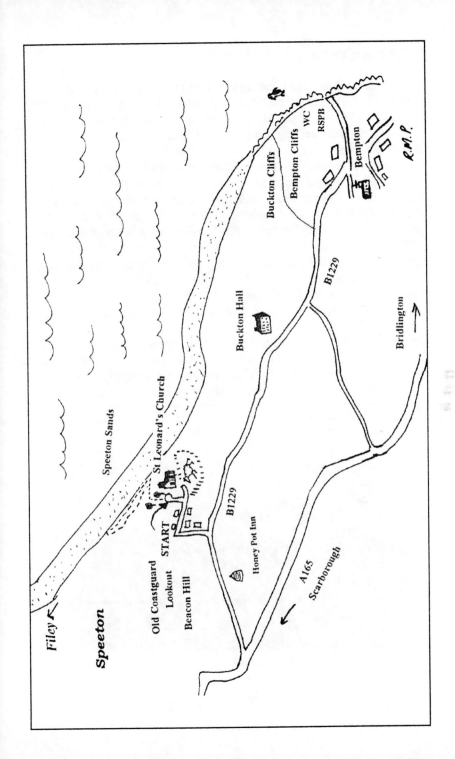

One of the smallest, most primitive churches in Yorkshire, its registers go back to 1638. It is totally charming and seats only about 70 people. The plain font is Saxon and the Agnus Dei set into the wall opposite the door - a figure of a lamb bearing a cross - dates from 1120-25 and was found outside over the south door. Also in the north wall is a stone with a circular cross which is probably the original consecration cross of the church. Two trefoil headed recesses are set into the north wall, one with the carving of a Maltese cross. Outside again, look on the exterior south wall (the door side) for the sundial. On a sunny day, if you hold a pencil in the centre, you can tell the time. Charlotte visited St Leonard's at the end of May, 1852, when she was staying in Filey. Alone, she lodged with Mrs Smith again in the house in Belle Vue where she had stayed in 1849, accompanied by Ellen Nussey after Anne's death. Her month-long 1852 visit was her first to the coast since Anne's death, and it was undertaken for her health and as a pilgrimage to her younger sister Anne's grave in Scarborough.

On June 2nd 1852, Charlotte wrote to her father from Filey, describing St. Leonard's. The churches in the area at that time were dilapidated and run in a very inefficient manner. It is quite possible that sheep slept inside, for they wandered in to graze the grass which grew between the floor bricks.

The tiny Speeton Church, which Charlotte visited in 1852.

In the same letter Charlotte described her amusement when she attended a service at St Leonard's. 'On Sunday afternoon I went to a church which I should like Mr Nicholls to see' (this reference was to Arthur Nicholls, her father's curate, who she would marry two years later in 1854). 'It was certainly not more than thrice the length and breadth of our passage, floored with brick, the walls green with mould, the pews painted white, but the paint almost worn off with time and decay. At one end there is a little gallery for the singers, and when these personages stood up to perform, they all turned their backs upon the congregation, and the congregation turned their backs upon pulpit and parson. The effect of this manouevre was so ludicrous, I could hardly help laughing; had Mr Nicholls been there he certainly would have laughed out. Looking up at the gallery and seeing only the broad backs of the singers presented to their audience was excessively grotesque'.

After exploring the church, begin your walk at the stile by the trees near the entrance to the gravel parking area. Follow the path 50 yards to a second stile and then go diagonally across a field to yet another stile. Continue right and left on the obvious path and very soon you'll get a view of Filey and Bempton Cliffs; to my mind, one of the most wonderful views on this coast. Make your way down, passing a wooden bench. Further down, at a perfect viewpoint, there's a stone seat - a monument to a young Dutch vet. who worked for a while in Bridlington. She loved this place, facing her home country across the North Sea. I was lucky to be in her company on this very walk once but, sadly, she died in a car accident one Christmas Eve. The descent by steps from here to the beach is very steep. Go no further if you can't face the climb back! The beach itself is delightful and often deserted. If you face south, the mighty and dazzling chalk bastion of Bempton cliffs towers before you, at around 500 feet the highest point of this coast. Sometimes, in the reflected sunset, they are a wonderful rose colour. This is where the wolds, the backbone of East Yorkshire, finally meet the sea. Linger a while to wonder at nature's grandeur. If you have a bent for geology, in the Speeton clay and red chalk down here, ammonites and belemnites are to be found. Return by the same route, a very steep climb, pausing often to take in the views and to rest.

§

Walk 5
Cliff House, Filey Brigg, St Oswald's Church
4 miles, 2½ hours - medium steep

Filey is, and always was, a quieter resort than either Scarborough or Bridlington. There was less space to expand, and perhaps when its spa well dried up last century, the visitors did likewise. Its name is thought to have come from various sources, and is spelt in the Domesday Book, 'Fuielac' or 'Fiuelac'. There are many interpretations of the meaning of this, ranging from five lakes (there were certainly many pools down in the old ravine) to five woods. The old Northumbrian word for wood was 'lah', and at that time there was a forest which stretched from Scalby to Filey. Others say the name comes from the brigg resembling a file running out to sea. The 'Brigg' of Filey Brigg could have come from the Roman name for the headland, which was Brigantium Extremum (the furthest point of land occupied by the old Brigante tribe) or from the old name for a bridge. The Romans built a signal station around the 4th century, on Carr Naze. There was a chain of these lookout cum beacon stations along the east coast, to warn of invaders.

Start this walk in Belle Vue Street, near the sea end, outside the house which was Mrs Smith's lodgings where Charlotte Brontë stayed on two occasions. The first was in 1849 with Ellen Nussey after Anne's death in Scarborough. On the second, in 1852, she was alone. You will see the plaque on the wall. During their stay there would have been a sea view from the house, as the town was not quite fully developed as a resort. Continue walking east to the pub on the corner and then turn left and walk along in front of a row of smart apartments. Pause on the lawn here to get a good view of Filey Brigg to the north. Ahead you will encounter the Information Centre in the Town Council complex. Turn right down the steep cobbled continuation of Murray Street which is called Cargate Hill.

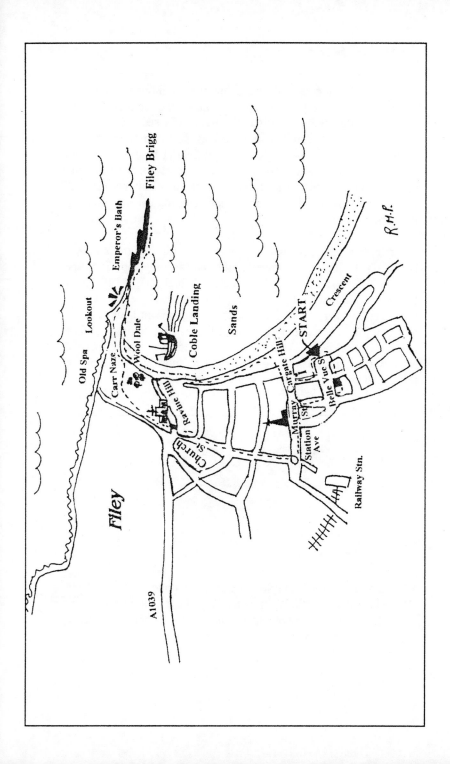

Follow this down towards the beach and the small funfair. Turn left at the bottom, cross the road and walk alongside the sea wall until you reach the lifeboat station. Here you will see a unique and colourful scene - a row of fishing 'cobles' lined up on the sloping coble landing in all their glory. These fishing boats are still an essential part of the local economy. Very early in the morning, tractors haul them down to the sea to seek their summer catch of lobster and crab, or in the winter, their longline catch of cod and haddock.

The attractively shaped coble is peculiar to the Yorkshire coast and is thought to be a descendant of the Viking longship. Even the modern diesel-powered coble resembles its forebears. It has a high bow, a deep forefoot, a flat bottom and no keel, and the flat transom stern slopes sharply. The long rudder is dropped in after push-off and acts as a keel, and then the tiller is slotted into it. The overlapping 'clinker' planks used to be made from larch and the main timbers from oak. If you arrive in the morning, you may see the cobles coming into shore, stern first.

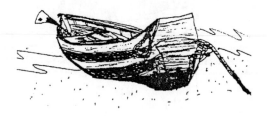

Walk onto Filey sands and follow the shore along past the Sailing Club which is in a little Wyke called Wool Dale. Ahead of you are the high cliffs consisting of boulder clay, protected below by a ledge of coralline oolite. Fossils are to be found here.

Walk along until you see a way up onto the lower Brigg but beware of the tide. **Don't** go to the end of the Brigg if the tide is coming in or washing over it. Many lives have been lost here by huge waves snatching people from the rock walkway.

Filey Brigg is quite spectacular. It protects Filey from the northerly winds. For the geologically inclined, it is a mile-long ridge of lower calcereous grit There is a story that a pier of stone built by the Romans runs south from it, called the Spitall. From the Brigg you get a clear view of Scarborough to the north. Look out for the large pools and caves, especially the Emperor's Bath. This lovely deep sandy rock pool is filled twice a day by the tide and stays full. It is said a Roman Emperor bathed here! Today boys sometimes dive for pennies.

Turn back and this time take the steep path up to the cliff top where you will get superb views of the coast. Near the coastguard's lookout, look for the remains of the Roman signal station, first excavated in 1857. Walk back towards the town through North Cliff Country Park via a sealed road called Centenary Way.

Just after the park exit you will see a sign to St. Oswald's Church. Make a diversion and visit the church which has a multitude of wonderful Early English features. Charlotte explored it in 1849 and 1852. Here, she found sheep grazing on grass which grew between the floor cobbles and a preacher who she considered slightly crazy. The church, which has a fish for a weather vane, dates from 1180 and was probably built by the Augustinians from Bridlington Priory. The South Door is an excellent example of Norman work, the font dates from the origins of the church, and the stone altar in the sanctuary is especially interesting . It is a 'sealed altar', containing a receptacle for the bones of saints or other relics. The stone effigy in the south wall is a memorial to a Boy Bishop and was installed just after 1250. Near here is the recently added Fishermen's Memorial and window, commemorating those lost at sea. The Priest's door is a good example of Early English design and the Chancel windows are also Early English. A walk around the outside the church is also very rewarding.

Note the belfry windows, the lovely tower, the tower staircase on the south side, the lean on the south-west buttress and the numerous carved heads. Outside the west end is a tiny window, and just above the Mass clock on the side is an unusual bronze sun dial. The Greek inscription means 'The Night Cometh'.

When you leave the church gate you will see a small pedestrian bridge to your left through the trees. Cross this, over Ravine Road, and you will find yourself in Church Street. When it ends, cross directly into Station Road and at the big roundabout turn left into Station Avenue. This will soon become Murray Street, the main shopping street, which will lead you back to the Information Centre, and Cliff House.

§

The stained glass window in St Oswald's Church, which is part of the Memorial to celebrate the tradition of fishing in Filey.

56

Chapter 4
Filey, 1852
Charlotte Visits Alone

Three years had passed since that desolate May when Charlotte had buried Anne in Scarborough. Although now a successful and celebrated novelist, still writing under the pseudonym 'Currer Bell', Charlotte was lonely and depressed. Her father had become withdrawn and the parsonage was a quiet and lonely place. She was in poor health, brought on by her depression, and often she would beg Ellen Nussey to come to visit Haworth in order to lift her spirits. During 1851 and 1852, she had travelled around England to escape her loneliness, visiting various friends. This included Mrs Gaskell, (who later wrote her famous biography of Charlotte) in Manchester and her publishers in London. She visited Brookroyd, Ellen's home, in February 1852 but her illness persisted and she found it impossible to get down to finishing 'Villette', the novel about her Brussels experiences which she had begun in June, 1851. The first part was completed but could get no further. For four months she did not lift her pen, except to write letters. Eventually, in May, 1852, she decided to heed her doctor's advice and take a holiday at the seaside. He recommended that the bracing sea air of Scarborough or Bridlington would do her the world of good. Initially Scarborough had been her planned destination but when she discovered that Miss Wooler, her old friend, wouldn't be going until later in the season, Charlotte changed her mind. While she intended to make a pilgrimage to Anne's grave and check the headstone that she had ordered for it, she could not face staying alone in Scarborough, a place which held such sad memories for her.

Instead, she returned to Mrs Smith's house in Filey where she had stayed with Ellen in 1849. She arrived within a few days of the anniversary of Anne's death (28th May). On 4th June she went to Anne's grave in St Mary's graveyard in Scarborough. Finding five mistakes in all on the engraved memorial stone, she arranged for it to be replaced. But the engravers still managed to get it wrong and, to this day, Anne's age at her death is stated as 28. She was 29.

The town had changed a lot since her last visit. The Scarborough to Bridlington branch railway line was open and, just that year, gas lighting had been installed in Filey. And The Crescent, a grand curve of housing on the highest point overlooking the sea, was just being developed by the architect Unett.

Although the weather in early June was at first cold, Charlotte wrote a purposefully cheery letter to her father dated June 2nd. 'On the whole I get on very well here, but I have not bathed yet, as I am told it is much too cold and early in the season. The Sea is very grand. Yesterday it was a somewhat unusually high tide - and I stood about an hour on the cliffs yesterday afternoon - watching the tumbling in of great tawny turbid waves - that made the whole shore white with foam and filled the air with a sound hollower and deeper than thunder. There are so very few visitors at Filey yet - that I and a few sea-birds and fishing-boats have often the whole expanse of sea, shore and cliff to ourselves - When the tide is out - the sands are wide - long and smooth and very pleasant to walk on. When the high tides are in - not a vestige of sand remains....' This is an apt description of Filey beach today. She wrote to Ellen... 'They (the Smiths) seemed glad to see me - remembered you and me very well, and seemingly, with great goodwill...Filey seems to me much altered; - more lodging

Filey Brigg

58

houses, some of them very handsome - have been built; - the sea has all its own grandeur - I walk on the sands a good deal, and try not to feel desolate and melancholy. How sorely my heart longs for you, I need not say. I have bathed once - it seemed to do me good ...One day I set out with intent to trudge to Filey Bridge, (Brigg) but was frightened back by two cows. I mean to try again...'

Charlotte stayed a whole month in Filey. In a letter to Miss Wooler she was more truthful than to her father saying ...'The first week or ten days - I greatly feared the sea-side would not suit me - for I suffered almost constantly from head-ache and other harrassing ailments; the weather too was dark, stormy and excessively- bitterly cold; my Solitude, under such circumstances, partook of the character of Desolation; I had some dreary evening-hours and night-vigils'.

Charlotte was something of a hypochondriac but a letter to Ellen from Filey revealed that what she really feared was that the illness which had dogged her the previous winter may be returning. She mentioned pain in the right side and hip, in the middle of the chest and 'burning and aching between the shoulders'. Ellen had previously advised her to take a doctor's advice and walk for three or four hours a day. Charlotte heeded the advice and wrote ....'accordingly I have walked as much as I could since I came here, and look almost as sunburnt and weather-beaten as a fisherman or a bathing-woman with being out in the open air.'

She attended St Oswald's Church in Filey and wrote to her father... 'There is a well meaning but utterly inactive clergyman at Filey, and methodists flourish.' Methodism was indeed taking a hold amongst fishing folk in Bridlington and Filey at this time, although some unwelcome preachers had been pelted with fish in Bridlington! The churches in the area at that time were certainly dilapidated and run in a very inefficient manner. It is quite possible that sheep slept inside, and they certainly wandered in to graze the grass which grew between the floor bricks.

Filey as it is today. Note the grand crescents of houses. The building of these began at the time of Charlotte's second visit.

One Sunday she attended a church service in a church which she described with some relish and amusement to her father. It is possible that it is St Oswald's Church in Filey, which she certainly visited, but more likely the description fits the tiny Norman church of St Leonard's at Speeton, further south along the coast. .... 'On Sunday afternoon I went to a church which I should like Mr Nicholls to see.... (this reference was to be the first sign that she may be showing some interest in Arthur Bell Nicholls, her father's curate who she would marry two years later in 1854)....It was certainly not more than thrice the length and breadth of our passage, floored with brick, the walls green with mould, the pews painted white, but the paint almost worn off with time and decay. At one end there is a little gallery for the singers, and when these personages stood up to perform, they all turned their backs upon the congregation, and the congregation turned their backs upon pulpit and parson. The effect of this manoeuvre was so ludicrous I could hardly help laughing; had Mr Nicholls been there he certainly would have laughed out. Looking up at the gallery and seeing only the broad backs of the singers presented to their audience was excessively grotesque'. There is no sign of there ever having been a gallery in St. Leonard's, but Charlotte may have been referring to the type of raised singers' pew which was common at that time.

After the Filey visit, she was to reflect in a letter to Smith Williams that ..... 'the warm weather and a visit to the sea have done me much good physically;' but she also admitted that .... 'I have recovered neither elasticity of animal spirits nor flow of the power of composition.' She returned to Haworth at the end of June and for two weeks worked steadily on her novel *'Villette'*. But then her father had a mild stroke and she had no choice but to nurse him. Her work was interrupted again and there were more minor setbacks and bouts of depression. Ellen Nussey, who had been four months in Sussex, returned to Yorkshire and visited Charlotte in October. Cheered up by her visit, Charlotte put her head down and

St Oswald's Church, Filey.

61

by November she had completed *'Villette'*, which was to be her final work. Publication came at the end of January 1853 and, for the first time, it was under her own name. The novel was well-received and all reviews were favourable. It made her famous in her own right, although 'Currer Bell' was, of course, already acclaimed.

Now that the pressure of completing the novel was at last over, her health improved some more. In February she wrote...'December, January, February, '51-52, passed like a long stormy night, conscious of one painful dream, all solitary grief and sickness. The corresponding months of '52-53 have gone over my head quietly and not uncheerfully. Thank God for the change and the repose! My father too has borne the season well; and my book and its reception thus far, have pleased and cheered him.'

But another important phase in Charlotte's life was developing. On 13th December 1852, Arthur Nicholls, an Irishman, her father's curate for over seven years, proposed. Over the years Charlotte had had no interest whatsoever in him, although she'd inserted him as a decent character at the end of *'Shirley'* - a Mr Macarthy, the fourth curate. For some time she'd suspected that he may be holding a candle for her. When he earnestly asked her to marry him that evening, she described him to Ellen thus... 'Shaking from head to foot, looking deadly pale, speaking low, vehemently yet with difficulty - he made me for the first time feel what it costs a man to declare affection where he doubts response....he spoke of sufferings he had borne for months..'

This was not the first proposal Charlotte had received; she had received three already, but this was the most significant. Charlotte promised to give him her response the next day. When she did, it was in the negative. Her father had been so infuriated by what he considered the cheek of Nicholls, that she said she could do nothing else. But, secretly, she was still unsure as to her own feelings, so her refusal gave her valuable time to think.

§

Chapter 5
Hornsea, 1853
Charlotte Visits Miss Wooler

In 1853, after the publication of *'Villette'* in January, Charlotte was still being pursued by Arthur Nicholls, her father's curate, who had proposed to her in December 1852. Since the ageing and possessive Patrick had opposed the liaison, thinking his daughter deserved better, a great deal of tension had built up in the parsonage. Perhaps it was this very opposition which ignited Charlotte's interest in someone who had been around for so long, in addition to the loneliness which she had endured since the loss of her sisters.

Charlotte spent time in London during the early part of the year, relieved to escape her father's anger. But Patrick's vitriol at the curate's presumptuousness continued (the fact that Arthur had not even asked the Reverend Brontë's permission to propose to his daughter riled him). Her father wrote savage letters to Charlotte in London about Nicholls, insinuating that Charlotte may have encouraged him. Back at home, Charlotte found Haworth unbearable again. Fed up, Nicholls applied to be a missionary in Australia, planning to leave Haworth in May. He handed in his notice but by April he'd decided this was not the answer. However, his notice still stood and he still intended to leave his post. By now Patrick was not speaking to his curate, so Charlotte fled again, this time to Manchester to see her friend Mrs Elizabeth Gaskell.

She returned home, and on 25th May, Nicholls' curacy came to an end. He departed and soon took up a post at Kirk Smeaton near Pontefract. The strain took its toll on Charlotte and she fell ill. In his absence she began to realise even more how solitary her life had become and slowly the seeds of her decision to defy her father and actually marry Arthur Nicholls took root. The still single Ellen disapproved, probably from jealousy at the thought of this threat to their longstanding friendship, but this only served to make Charlotte keener still.

She was annoyed with her friend, and considered her two-faced, for Ellen herself had recently hoped to receive a proposal from her friend's brother, although it never eventuated.

In July, 1853, Arthur returned to the area, staying in Oxenhope, and they met without Patrick's knowledge. Romance was in the air.

In August Charlotte set out for a holiday in Scotland with her friends the Taylors, but her first trip across the border was cut short after a few days when they decided to return and spend a few days in Ilkley in Yorkshire instead, due to the illness of the couple's baby. In all, she was only away a week. It was at this time that Charlotte began to plan another visit to the Yorkshire coast. She returned to Ilkley for a further few days, this time with her old friend and teacher, Miss Margaret Wooler. As they walked the avenues, she told her about her feelings involving both Ellen and Arthur Nicholls and Miss Wooler kindly invited her to stay with her in Hornsea, a resort which lies east of Hull in East Yorkshire.

The house at 94 Newbegin, Hornsea, where Charlotte Brontë stayed with Miss Wooler in 1853, as it looks today.

64

But before she could go to Hornsea, Mrs Gaskell came to visit Charlotte for the first time. She stayed four days and during this time Charlotte told her how her father had nipped the proposal from Arthur Nicholls in the bud. This was to cause Mrs Gaskell to say in her biography later on that Patrick still treated Charlotte like a child and that he was a tyrant who had prevented his daughters marrying. However, it is more likely that Charlotte still had some doubts about whether she could face being married to the sombre Arthur Nicholls, so it was not entirely her father's fault. With her own income, she could easily have defied Patrick much earlier.

At the end of August, Charlotte wrote to her friend Miss Wooler who was by now renting rooms at No 94 Newbegin in Hornsea ... 'All the summer I felt the wish and cherished the intention to join you for a brief period at the seaside, nor do I yet relinquish the purpose, though its fulfilment must depend on my father's health.' It wasn't until the end of September that she finally managed to get away to stay in Hornsea for a week. Hornsea was a quiet place, known for its healthy waters, and was popular with well-off Hull holidaymakers, although the railway link didn't open until 1864. The house at 94 Newbegin had been purpose built around 1850 as a seaside lodging house, like the other six houses in the terrace. It had a balcony and was in pseudo Swiss style, the exterior coated with stucco. Indeed, the address was then known as No. 4 Swiss Terrace. The family at present in residence have sympathetically restored the house, which is on a main road leading towards the sea. As yet there is no plaque on the wall.

During her stay Charlotte took pleasant strolls on the sands and, accompanied by Miss Wooler, walked beside Hornsea Mere, the largest natural lake in Yorkshire. The lake wasn't opened for pleasure boating or fishing until 1890 but it was always a popular walking spot, noted especially for its sunsets. While Miss Wooler, who Charlotte had known since their pupil/teacher and teaching days together, had never become the intimate friend that Ellen was, she was nevertheless an intelligent companion who had supported Charlotte since schooldays through all the tragedies which had dogged her life so far.

This holiday in Hornsea was to be Charlotte's last in England, so it was fortunate that it was a happy one. Even an unpleasant incident which occurred on her way back from Hornsea to Hull by coach was treated with good humour. She wrote to Miss Wooler on her return ... 'a respectable-looking woman and her little girl were admitted into the coach. The child...had not sat long before - without any previous warning, or the slightest complaint of nausea - sickness seized her and the contents of her little stomach - consisting apparently of a milk breakfast - were unceremoniously deposited in my lap! Of course, I alighted from the coach in a pretty mess, but succeeded in procuring water and a towel at the station (Hull), with which I managed to make my dress and cloak more presentable.'

Charlotte was most grateful to Miss Wooler. In the same letter she said... 'The week I spent at Hornsea was a happy and pleasant week. Thank you, my dear Miss Wooler - for the true kindness which gave it its chief charm. I shall think of you often, especially when I walk out - and during the long evenings. I believe the weather has at length taken a turn; today it is beautifully fine. I wish I were at Hornsea and just now preparing to go out with you for a walk on the sands or along the lake.'

Mrs Gaskell, after her stay in Haworth in mid-September, was meanwhile busy match-making. Knowing that one of Patrick's objections to Charlotte's marriage was Arthur Nicholls' low income, she began to engineer a pension for the clergyman from charitable funds. It was eventually awarded to Arthur.

In November 1852, another significant event occurred. Charlotte had intended to visit London to see her publishers but she discovered that George Smith, of Smith, Elder & Co. was to be married. She had always harboured a notion that perhaps she may marry him, so maybe this event triggered what followed. Feeling betrayed, she cancelled her trip to London, wrote briefly to congratulate him, and abandoned herself to deep loneliness. And then, after a period of heartsearching, she decided to give Arthur a chance.

She admitted to her father that she had been writing to Arthur for the past 6 months and demanded that they be allowed to get to know each other. Charlotte, once her mind was made up, rarely took no for an answer. Patrick reluctantly agreed. The atmosphere at the parsonage lifted immediately. Charlotte even resumed her correspondence with Ellen. On 3rd April 1854, Nicholls was allowed to come to stay at Haworth. He stayed a few days and this is when plans were laid down. It was decided that he would come back to Haworth as curate, they would marry, and he would live at the parsonage because Charlotte had to look after her father. And so the engagement was decided upon and the future decreed, not by Patrick, but by Charlotte.

The marriage took place in Haworth Church on 29th June 1854. Only Miss Wooler and Ellen were invited although others came to watch. The Rev. Sutcliffe Sowden, a friend of Arthur Nicholls', officiated. The ceremony took place at eight in the morning - Charlotte dressed simply in white muslin, her bonnet trimmed with green leaves. It was left to Miss Wooler to give Charlotte away because Patrick had decided the night before ,with his usual awkwardness, that he would not attend the ceremony. The honeymoon was spent in Ireland, Arthur's homeland. On the journey to the west of Ireland they stopped in Wales and in Dublin, where Arthur had attended Trinity College. Charlotte caught cold in Wales and by the time they reached Banagher, Nicholls' former home, she needed a week to recover. Charlotte was impressed by Arthur's family, who were quite middle class and not the peasants that her father had hinted at. They continued their tour to Limerick and Kilkee, where Charlotte revelled in the views of the Atlantic, and then went on to Tarbert, Tralee, Killarney and Cork.

They arrived back in Haworth on 2nd August and Charlotte settled down happily to married life.

§

Chapter 6
1854 - Charlotte's Death

The newly married Charlotte continued to write to Ellen Nussey, at first hinting that looking after two men was not really her cup of tea. But in fact she revelled in the 'busyness' of her role as a curate's wife and was truly happy and no longer lonely. She was finding married life more congenial than she'd imagined and wrote that Arthur was affectionate and caring. He was also sympathetic to her need for some precious time alone, and her thoughts were returning to a story she had begun called 'Willie Ellin'. But Arthur was less happy about her intimate letter writing to Ellen, and tension began to build over the friendship. Ellen was later to bitterly resent what she saw as the guarding of Charlotte by both Arthur and Patrick, which meant they hardly saw each other.

During the autumn, Charlotte was healthier than she had been for years. But at the end of November she took a walk with her husband to a waterfall on the moors and caught a bad cold in an unexpected downpour. Her cold and cough persisted through to January when, attacked by nausea, she suspected she was pregnant. She was, and severe morning sickness set in, so severe she became weak and emaciated. It persisted even after the first three months, becoming what doctors would now call *hyperaemesis gravidarum*. Despite a specialist's diagnosis that she would recover, she grew weaker. On 31st March,1855, three weeks before her 39th birthday, she died. The death certificate stated *phisis* (phthisis) which is consumption, but it was the pregnancy which killed her. She was buried in the family vault in Haworth (with all except Anne, who lay in Scarborough). Sadly, Charlotte had declined an invitation to visit Ellen in December, and the two had not met since September. But Ellen attended the funeral. And so the life of the last of the famous sisters also ended tragically and prematurely. Arthur Nicholls was to remain at Haworth with Patrick until the old man died in 1861. Arthur later married his cousin Mary in 1864. Ellen lived to the age of 80 and was an important source of information for Mrs Gaskell's invaluable biography of Charlotte.

§

Walk 6
Hornsea Mere
5 miles, 2½ hours - flat but mud.

This walk begins in the town of Hornsea. Bring your binoculars for bird-watching on the Mere. 252 bird species have been listed here. Never more than 9 feet deep, this 2 by 1 mile lake is the largest in Yorkshire and dates back to glacial times. Hornsea is a smaller town than Bridlington and Scarborough, but its earliest days as a resort can be traced back to 1730. Its chalybeate (iron salts) springs meant it also became a popular 'spa' town. The first Marine Hotel was opened in 1837. In the 11th century the town belonged to the Abbey of St Mary's in York. The small stream which runs from the Mere to the sea was called Hornsea Beck before it was turned into Stream Dyke in 1785. Look out for unusual cobbled cottages.

Begin the walk at the Mereside car park down behind the Rose & Crown and the Victoria Hotel which are on Market Place. Walk north into Scalby Place and after 25 yards turn left into Back Westgate. On the corner you will see a restored cobbled cottage called Sunset Cottage. Look for the typical East Riding 'tumble gabling'. A few bits of cobble paving can be seen in front of the cottage too. At the corner of Back Westgate and Boroughbridge Lane, Quaker Cottage also has some cobbling in evidence. It was used as a meeting house in the 17th and 18th centuries. After 200 yards you will meet Westgate, a major road. On this junction is an 18th century farmhouse, 'The Pillars'. The old cobble Infants' School is next to it, built by Lady Strickland in 1845. It ceased to be a school in 1935 and is now called 'Mereton'.

Turn left here and cross the road onto the footpath. Continue straight along Seaton Road. Through the wood on your left you will catch glimpses of the Mere, close by. Continue for 1½ miles and you will see a strange round house on your right, which has square rooms inside. Follow the footpath past this round house for half a mile. Here you will see an interestingly patterned terracotta

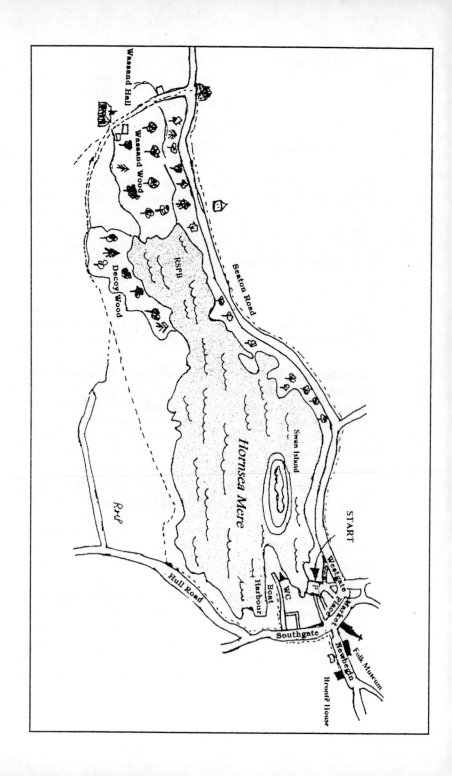

brick house on your right. Opposite this is a Y junction. Cross here and follow the tree-lined, gated road, passing a white cottage to your right. The road takes you through Wassand Woods which are a delight in springtime. You will soon come across the grounds of Wassand Hall and farm on the right. A chalybeate spring rose near here and Mr Constable of Wassand once oversaw a well where people came to 'take the waters' for a small charge. Its surroundings were planted with flowers and it existed until 1870, so Charlotte may very well have visited it and partaken of its 'cure'.

Bear left along the unmetalled road to a gate with a blue pointer on a yellow background. Follow these signs and you will eventually reach the main road on the other side of the Mere, on your left. On your right you will soon get a view of Wassand Hall, owned by the Strickland-Constables. It is private. There will be three further gates (with stiles) and then the footpath will go diagonally east across a field. Here you will see another stile with an anti-sheep gate and a narrow wooden bridge, then another stile, marked with a pointer. Cross another open field, another stile and the Mere should be 200 yards to your left, through a wood. Cross another open field and another stile. Now you will have a clear view of the Mere to your left. Continue along a long straight footpath between the cornfields

Hornsea Mere last century.

and a new hedge. At the end of the path, ignore the pointer and take a detour - a right turn up to the top of the ridge. From here you'll get great views of the Mere, Swan Island, and the distinctive red roofs of Hornsea. Follow the narrow path along the top of this ridge, and you'll see a well-signed path which goes over a stile. The path takes you down to Mere level and along its southern side to a five bar gate on the Hull Road. Turn left at the gate, and don't cross the road. Follow the footpath towards the town centre. At the Southgate junction you'll see a large boulder which once stood in the centre of the road and marked the boundary between Hornsea and Hornsea Burton. Turn left and carry on until you see a sign on your left pointing to the Mereside boating harbour and bird reserve. It is worth the diversion to take a wander down here. Come back another day if you want to go for a row on the lake in a hired rowing boat, one of the most relaxing things to do in Hornsea.

Once back on Southgate, look for a market cross dating from 1466 in front of the cemetery. This marks the site of the Thursday Market. Opposite the cross is Low Hall, a large farm building which was built in 1675 by Acklam. The garden was once a Quaker burial ground. Continuing along Southgate, part of the protected 'old town', take particular note of some wonderful Georgian houses, particularly Nos. 65, 66, 52 and 41-44, saved from demolition. Carry on to the traffic lights where you will see St Nicholas' Church. Built in 1442, it has some traces from the original Saxon church which was destroyed by Harold Hardrada in 1066 (in the lower crypt and tower). The original Market Cross from Market Place was moved into the churchyard in 1898. Carry on along Newbegin to No. 94, on the right, where Charlotte stayed with Miss Wooler (no plaque). There are two nice cafés nearby, one opposite and another slightly further up in a courtyard on the same side. If you have time, visit the excellent Folk Museum (once a farmhouse) at 11 Newbegin before returning to St. Nicholas' Church. Look for the Old Hall with its Dutch gabling in Market Place built in 1687 by Acklam. Return to the Mereside carpark via one of the snickets opposite the Church, or down Scalby Place.

§